HOW TO GET PAID FOR YOUR KNOWLEDGE:
TRY THE LATEST AND SIMPLEST TIPS

Adams H. Bells

Table of Contents

INTRODUCTION

A transformative guide that reveals the secrets of transforming your knowledge into tangible rewards is now available. In "How to Make Money from Your Knowledge: Try the Newest and Easiest Hints," we provide a straightforward guide to assist you in navigating the contemporary landscape, where your insights can generate income. This isn't simply a book; It is your entry into a world in which what you know becomes an asset of value.

Exploring the Information Economy

In a world immersed with data, your insight is cash ready to be spent. This book is your aide through the labyrinth of the information economy, offering experiences into transforming your ability into monetary achievement. From online stages to discussion standards, every section outfits you with commonsense procedures to flourish in the advanced age.

At its core, Simplicity and Innovation This book thrives on innovation and simplicity. We believe that the most efficient strategies are frequently the simplest, and adopting the most recent trends can open up new opportunities for monetizing your knowledge. Whether you're beginning or scaling, these standards are intended to be open and significant.

What You'll Find

1. Figuring out the Computerized Scene: Explore the internet based world with certainty, finding stages and devices to enhance your message.

2. Mastery of Content Creation: Release the force of convincing substance that resounds and creates pay.

3. Exchange and Estimating Techniques: Become the best at discussion and valuing for fair pay.

4. Scaling Your Insight Business: Investigate techniques to develop and thrive past constraints.

5. Keeping up with the Knowledge Economy: Embrace constant learning, advancement, and flexibility to lead in the developing information scene.

Set out on the Information Adaptation Excursion

As you read "How to Get Compensated with Your Insight," imagine a future where your skill isn't simply recognized yet celebrated. This book is your companion in the pursuit of knowledge wealth, whether you want to launch products, master online courses, or confidently negotiate.

Enter, look around, and allow the journey to begin. Your insight is your most noteworthy resource — we should open its maximum capacity together.

DISCLOSING YOUR ABILITY

In these pages, we'll dive profound into the most common way of disclosing your skill, figuring out its characteristic worth, and finding how to use it for both monetary benefit and individual satisfaction.

How to Use Your Expertise

Take a moment to think about yourself before beginning this investigation. Consider the interests that drive you, the abilities you've sharpened, and the encounters that have formed you. Your skill is a mosaic of these components, ready to be disclosed.

Make the effort to find the skills in your repertoire that can be sold. What are the requests of the market, and how do your capacities line up with these requirements? We'll explore the fragile harmony between seeking after what you love and perceiving amazing open doors for benefit.

Creating Your Special Selling Suggestion (USP)

The creation of a compelling Unique Selling Proposition (USP) is essential to demonstrating your expertise. Characterize what separates you in the tremendous scene of information. Why should people take your offer seriously?

Completely break down your interest group to fit your skill to their particular necessities. Laying out believability is principal, and we'll investigate different channels, from websites to digital recordings, where you might exhibit your insight and work at any point trust.

Noteworthy Stages

Putting forth clear objectives is the most vital phase in transforming your mastery into a productive endeavor. Characterize both present moment and long haul goals, illustrating what you intend to accomplish.

Make an individual stock that indexes your abilities, encounters, and accomplishments. This inventory provides a comprehensive overview of your individual expertise and serves as the foundation for your journey.

Focus on consistent learning. The scene of information is always advancing, and remaining refreshed guarantees your skill stays significant and important.

As you submerge yourself in this part, embrace the powerful idea of divulging your aptitude. This excursion isn't an agenda yet a groundbreaking interaction, laying the basis for a remunerating investigation of adapting what you know.

EXPLORING THE COMPUTERIZED SCENE

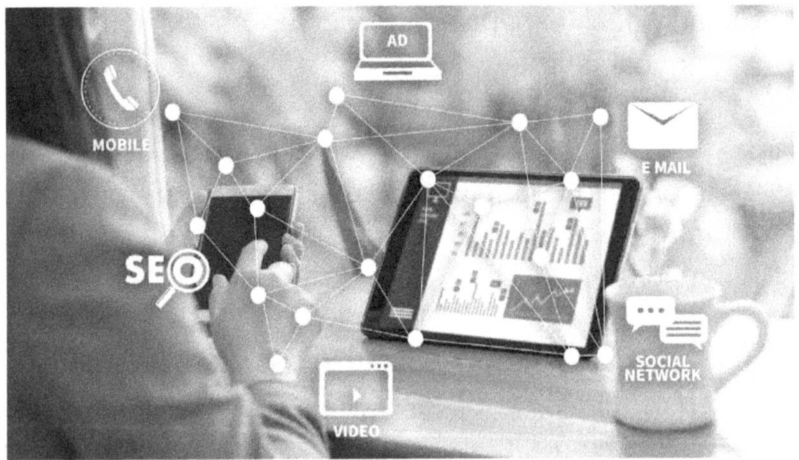

In the computerized age, the territory for adapting your insight is huge and always advancing. A well-thought-out strategy, familiarity with the tools at one's disposal, and proficiency with online platforms are all necessary for successfully navigating this landscape. We begin a comprehensive investigation of how to use the digital realm to expand your expertise and generate income in this chapter.

Figuring out the Advanced Scene

The Computerized Insurgency:
The advanced upset has on a very basic level changed how data is shared and consumed. We dive into the authentic setting, understanding the essential minutes that have molded the ongoing scene. From the appearance of the web to the ascent of online entertainment, handle the powers driving change.

Information Democratization:
The democratization of information is one of the major effects of the digital age. Investigate how obstructions to passage have been destroyed, giving phenomenal open doors to people to share their insight on a worldwide scale. Grasp the power elements at play in this democratized data biological system.

Methods for Making Yourself Known Online

Strengthening Your Online Presence:
Your excursion in the computerized scene starts with building a vigorous web-based presence. We explore the complexities of making a convincing individual brand on the web. From planning an easy to use site to upgrading virtual entertainment

profiles, get familiar with the fundamentals of laying out a computerized impression that spellbinds your crowd.

Content System for the Advanced Age:
In an ocean of computerized content, standing apart requires an essential substance approach. Jump into the subtleties of content creation, from making drawing in blog entries to delivering mixed media content. Reveal the insider facts of making content that illuminates as well as resounds with your ideal interest group.

Website optimization and Discoverability:
Figuring out the standards of Site design improvement (Search engine optimization) is vital for computerized achievement. Figure out how to advance your substance to upgrade discoverability. We demystify the universe of watchwords, meta labels, and backlinks, giving noteworthy experiences to support your internet based perceivability.

Web-based Entertainment Adaptation Strategies

Picking the Right Stages:
Not all virtual entertainment stages are made equivalent. Each has its interesting assets and

crowd socioeconomics. Take a look at the major platforms and choose those that complement your expertise. From Instagram to LinkedIn, tailor your way to deal with expand your effect.

Content Techniques for Online Entertainment:
A sophisticated content strategy is necessary because social media is a dynamic arena. Dig into the specialty of making content explicitly for every stage. Master the strategies that pique the interest of your audience and encourage them to participate, such as succinct messaging and compelling images.

Utilizing Social Media to Make Money:
Past preferences and offers, web-based entertainment can be a worthwhile road for adaptation. Reveal different adaptation strategies, from supported content to subsidiary advertising. Comprehend how to flawlessly incorporate income streams into your online entertainment presence without compromising credibility.

Internet business and Computerized Items

Sending off Your Own Advanced Items:
The digital environment makes it easy to launch and sell your own products. Investigate the

universe of computerized items, from digital books to online courses. Become familiar with the bit by bit course of conceptualizing, making, and advertising advanced items that take special care of the requirements of your crowd.

Internet business Stages and Apparatuses:
E-commerce platforms can be overwhelming to navigate. We guide you through the determination cycle, assisting you with picking the stage that lines up with your plan of action. From Shopify to Etsy, grasp the highlights and advantages of each.

Enhancing Your Business Channel:
A product's launch is only the beginning; streamlining your deals channel is the way to supported achievement. Investigate demonstrated procedures for driving traffic, changing over leads, and boosting your deals. Create a sales funnel that maximizes your revenue potential, from email marketing to upselling.

Dominating Web-based Courses

Planning Connecting with Courses:
Online courses offer a strong road for partaking top to bottom information. Jump into the craft of planning drawing in and viable web-based courses.

Grasp educational plan standards, sight and sound mix, and intelligent components that upgrade the growth opportunity.

Picking the Right Stage for Courses:
The huge number of online course stages can overpower. We separate the vital elements and contemplations to assist you with picking the stage that lines up with your course satisfied and ideal interest group.

Promoting Your Internet based Courses:
Indeed, even the most excellent courses need successful showcasing. Take a look at a wide range of marketing options for your online courses, from buzz about the launch to ongoing marketing efforts. Figure out how to fabricate expectation and drive enlistments.

Advice on Freelancing

Exploring Independent Stages:
For freelancers, the gig economy has opened up new opportunities. We investigate famous independent stages, from Upwork to Fiverr, and

guide you through the method involved with making a convincing profile. Learn how to stand out in a market that is full of competitors.

Getting Lucrative Gigs:
It's not enough to just get any gig when you freelance; you need to get high-paying gigs as well. Learn discussion procedures, estimating models, and strategies to situate yourself as an exceptional specialist. Improve your freelancing skills by setting rates and providing exceptional value.

Constructing Long haul Independent Connections:
Rehash business is the soul of outsourcing achievement. Find how to construct long haul associations with clients. We dig into successful correspondence, project the executives, and client fulfillment techniques that encourage continuous coordinated efforts.

Strategies for Pricing and Negotiation

How to Determine Your Worth:
Setting the right cost for your skill is a fragile equilibrium. Comprehend how to decide your value by considering elements, for example, experience, market interest, and rivalry. This segment engages you to convey your worth unhesitatingly.

Viable Discussion Methods:
The art of negotiation can have a significant impact on your earnings. Investigate powerful discussion strategies that outcome in commonly advantageous arrangements. Master the skills that make you a skilled negotiator, such as understanding the requirements of the client and setting boundaries.

Making Things Work for Both Parties:
Effective talks are tied in with making mutual benefit circumstances. Figure out how to structure bargains that benefit both you and your clients. The key to developing long-term, positive relationships is striking a balance between assertiveness and compromise.

Scaling Your Insight Business

Robotization and Assignment:
Scaling your insight business requires vital utilization of mechanization and designation. Explore the art of delegation and identify repetitive tasks that can be automated to free up your time for high-impact activities.

Organizing a Team:

As your business extends, building a group becomes fundamental. Comprehend the critical jobs to consider while building a group, whether it's menial helpers, content makers, or client care. Figure out how to lead and motivate your group to add to your business' prosperity.

Diversifying sources of revenue:
Depending on a solitary revenue stream can be hazardous. Investigate systems for broadening your income streams. From subsidiary advertising to counseling administrations, find extra roads for creating pay and shielding your monetary solidness.

Keeping up with the Knowledge Economy

Adjusting to Mechanical Advances:
The information economy is innately attached to mechanical headways. Remain ahead by grasping arising advances in your field. Whether it's man-made consciousness, blockchain, or increased reality, handle what these advancements can mean for your skill.

Professional growth and continuous learning:
In a quickly evolving scene, ceaseless learning isn't simply helpful however vital. Investigate roads for

proficient turn of events, from online courses to industry meetings. Remain at the front of your field to keep up with significance and skill.

Systems administration and Joint effort:
Organizing stays a foundation of progress. Develop significant associations inside your industry. Investigate cooperative open doors that grow your scope and acquaint you with new crowds. From online discussions to industry occasions, uncover the force of key systems administration.

BUILDING AN INDIVIDUAL BRAND

Defining Personal Branding

Personal branding is more than just a logo or a tagline; it's the collective perception people have about you. We delve into the essence of personal branding, exploring how it goes beyond a professional facade to embody your values, expertise, and the unique qualities that make you who you are.

The Power of Perception

Perception shapes reality, especially in the digital realm. We explore the psychology of perception and how intentional branding efforts can influence the way others perceive you. Understand how to craft a narrative that aligns with your goals and resonates with your audience.

Authenticity in Personal Branding

Authenticity is the cornerstone of a powerful personal brand. We discuss the importance of staying true to yourself and how authenticity builds trust with your audience. Discover how to showcase your genuine self while maintaining a professional image.

Crafting Your Unique Brand Identity

Identifying Your Core Values

Your core values form the foundation of your brand identity. We guide you through a self-discovery process to identify the principles that matter most to you. Learn how to align your personal values with your brand, creating a cohesive and authentic identity.

Defining Your Unique Selling Proposition (USP)

In a crowded digital space, standing out requires a clear and compelling USP. We explore how to define your USP—what makes you unique and why people should pay attention. This section guides you through the process of identifying and emphasizing your distinctive strengths.

Visual Branding

Visual elements are powerful tools for brand recall. From selecting a color palette to designing a logo, we break down the key components of visual branding. Understand how to create a cohesive and visually appealing brand identity that leaves a lasting impression.

Crafting Your Brand Story

Every brand has a story, and yours is no exception. We delve into the art of storytelling, helping you craft a narrative that connects with your audience on a deeper level. Discover how to share your journey, challenges, and successes in a way that resonates.

Building an Online Presence

Creating a User-Friendly Website

Your website is often the first point of contact with your audience. We guide you through the process of creating a user-friendly and visually appealing website. Explore essential elements, from an engaging homepage to a seamless navigation experience.

Optimizing Social Media Profiles

Social media is a powerful tool for personal branding. We delve into the nuances of optimizing your social media profiles across platforms. From choosing the right profile picture to crafting compelling bios, learn how to present a consistent and professional image.

Blogging and Content Creation

Blogging is not just a platform for sharing knowledge; it's a key component of personal branding. We explore the art of blogging, from choosing topics that align with your brand to writing in a voice that reflects your personality. Learn how to use content creation as a tool for brand building.

Engaging with Your Audience

Building a personal brand is not a one-way street. We discuss the importance of engaging with your audience authentically. Explore strategies for responding to comments, participating in discussions, and creating a sense of community around your brand.

Building Credibility and Authority

Showcasing Expertise

Credibility is built on a foundation of expertise. We explore effective ways to showcase your knowledge and skills. From creating insightful content to participating in industry discussions, learn how to position yourself as an authority in your field.

Collaborations and Partnerships

Collaborations can amplify your brand's reach and credibility. We guide you through the process of identifying potential collaborators and establishing mutually beneficial partnerships. Understand how to leverage the networks of others to enhance your brand's authority.

Client Testimonials and Case Studies

Nothing speaks louder than satisfied clients. We explore the power of client testimonials and case studies in building credibility. Learn how to gather and showcase testimonials that highlight the impact of your work.

Consistency and Adaptability

Maintaining Consistency Across Platforms

Consistency is key in personal branding. We discuss the importance of maintaining a consistent image and messaging across all platforms. Explore how to create a cohesive brand experience that reinforces your identity.

Adapting to Evolving Trends

The digital landscape is dynamic, and trends evolve. We explore the importance of staying adaptable while maintaining the core elements of your brand. Learn how to embrace change without compromising the authenticity of your personal brand.

Handling Brand Evolution

As you grow and evolve, so should your brand. We discuss strategies for handling brand evolution, whether it's a shift in focus, a rebrand, or a change in messaging. Discover how to navigate these transitions while maintaining the trust of your audience.

Monetizing Your Personal Brand

Exploring Monetization Avenues

Your personal brand can be a valuable asset for generating income. We explore various monetization avenues, from sponsored content to affiliate marketing. Understand how to seamlessly integrate revenue streams into your personal brand strategy.

Creating and Selling Products

Your brand can extend beyond services to include products. We guide you through the process of creating and selling products that align with your brand. From e-books to merchandise, explore diverse options for product creation.

Building a Premium Brand

Positioning your brand as premium requires strategic efforts. We discuss the elements that contribute to a premium brand, from high-quality content to exclusive offerings. Learn how to convey value and command premium pricing.

Measuring and Adjusting

Key Performance Indicators (KPIs)

To gauge the effectiveness of your personal branding efforts, it's crucial to track key performance indicators. We explore relevant KPIs, from website traffic to social media engagement. Understand how to interpret these metrics and make informed adjustments.

Feedback and Iteration

Feedback is a valuable tool for improvement. Learn how to gather feedback from your audience and peers. Explore the iterative process of refining your personal brand based on insights and evolving goals.

Reputation Management

Your reputation is a vital aspect of your personal brand. We discuss strategies for reputation management, including addressing criticism, handling controversies, and maintaining a positive online presence.

CONTENT CREATION AUTHORITY

In the digital age, where information saturates every corner of the internet, mastering the art of content creation is a fundamental skill for those seeking to monetize their knowledge. This chapter is a deep dive into the intricacies of content creation, offering insights, strategies, and practical tips to empower you to produce content that not only informs but captivates and resonates with your audience.

Understanding the Essence of Content Creation

Content creation is more than a mere act; it's a strategic process of crafting valuable and engaging materials for your audience. In this section, we delve into the definition of content creation and explore how it serves as the cornerstone of your online presence and brand.

The Role of Content in the Digital Landscape

To navigate the vast digital landscape, understanding the role of content is crucial. We discuss how content serves as the bridge between you and your audience, establishing connections, building trust, and ultimately driving the success of your knowledge business.

Types of Content

Content comes in various forms, each with its unique strengths. From written articles and blog posts to videos, podcasts, and infographics, we explore the diverse landscape of content types. Discover which formats align best with your expertise and audience.

Crafting Engaging and Valuable Content

Identifying Your Audience's Needs

The foundation of compelling content is a deep understanding of your audience's needs. Learn how to conduct audience research, identify pain points, and tailor your content to provide solutions and value. This section sets the stage for content that resonates.

Developing a Content Strategy

A well-defined content strategy is the backbone of effective content creation. We guide you through the process of developing a strategy that aligns with your business goals. From editorial calendars to theme planning, discover how to create a roadmap for consistent and purposeful content.

The Art of Storytelling

Storytelling is a powerful tool for content creators. We explore the art of crafting narratives that capture attention and evoke emotions. Understand the key elements of a compelling story and learn how to weave storytelling into your content for maximum impact.

Creating Evergreen Content

While trends come and go, evergreen content stands the test of time. Explore the importance of creating content with enduring value. From comprehensive guides to timeless principles, learn how to produce content that remains relevant and continues to attract audiences.

Optimizing for Search Engines and Discoverability

Introduction to SEO

Search Engine Optimization (SEO) is a cornerstone of online visibility. Gain a comprehensive introduction to SEO, understanding how it works and why it's crucial for content creators. From keywords to meta tags, grasp the essentials of optimizing your content for search engines.

Keyword Research and Implementation

Effective SEO starts with strategic keyword research. We delve into the process of identifying relevant keywords for your content and implementing them seamlessly. Understand how to strike the right balance between optimization and natural language.

On-Page and Off-Page SEO

SEO is a multifaceted strategy that extends beyond keywords. Explore both on-page and off-page SEO techniques. From optimizing your content structure to building backlinks, learn how to enhance your content's visibility across search engines.

Local SEO for Targeted Audiences

For those targeting local audiences, local SEO is a game-changer. Discover how to optimize your content for local search, from creating location-specific content to leveraging Google My Business. This section provides insights into reaching and engaging local audiences.

Visual Content Creation

The Power of Visuals

Visual content holds a unique allure for audiences. We explore why visuals matter and how they can enhance your content. From infographics to images and videos, understand how to leverage visual elements to communicate effectively.

Graphic Design Basics

Creating visually appealing content doesn't always require a design background. We provide a primer on graphic design basics, offering practical tips and tools to elevate the visual appeal of your content. Uncover the secrets to creating eye-catching graphics.

Video Content Creation

Video is a dynamic and engaging medium for content creators. We guide you through the process of creating compelling videos, from scripting to editing. Learn about different video formats, platforms, and techniques to make your video content stand out.

Podcasting Essentials

Podcasts offer a unique way to connect with your audience. Explore the essentials of podcasting, from planning episodes to recording and editing. Learn how to optimize your podcast for discoverability and build a dedicated listener base.

Content Distribution and Promotion

Choosing the Right Distribution Channels

Creating content is just the first step; distributing it effectively is equally crucial. We discuss the various distribution channels available, from social media platforms to email newsletters. Discover how to choose the right channels for your audience.

Leveraging Social Media

Social media is a powerhouse for content distribution. We delve into strategies for leveraging different platforms, from crafting shareable content to engaging with your audience. Learn how to use social media to amplify the reach of your content.

Email Marketing for Content Promotion

Email marketing remains a potent tool for content promotion. Explore the intricacies of building an email list, crafting compelling newsletters, and driving engagement. Understand how to create a personalized and effective email marketing strategy.

Collaborations and Cross-Promotion

Collaborations with other content creators can expand your reach exponentially. We guide you through the process of collaborating and cross-promoting content. Learn how to identify potential collaborators and create mutually beneficial partnerships.

Measuring Content Performance

Analytics and Metrics Overview

To refine your content strategy, you need insights into performance. We provide an overview of key analytics and metrics, from website traffic to engagement rates. Understand how to interpret data and make informed decisions.

Tools for Content Analytics

Numerous tools are available to track and analyze content performance. We explore popular analytics tools and how to use them effectively. From Google Analytics to social media insights, learn how to harness these tools to refine your content strategy.

Iterative Content Improvement

Continuous improvement is the hallmark of successful content creators. We discuss the iterative process of refining and optimizing your content based on analytics and audience feedback. Understand how to adapt your strategy for continuous growth.

Content Monetization Strategies

Monetizing Through Ads

Advertisements can be a lucrative revenue stream for content creators. We explore different ad monetization models, from display ads to sponsored content. Understand how to integrate ads seamlessly into your content without compromising quality.

Affiliate Marketing Mastery

Affiliate marketing is a powerful way to earn commissions by promoting products or services. We guide you through the intricacies of affiliate marketing, from choosing the right products to creating compelling promotional content. Learn how to maximize earnings through strategic partnerships.

Selling Your Own Products

Your content can serve as a gateway to your products. We discuss strategies for creating and selling your own products, from e-books to merchandise. Understand how to align your products with your content and create a seamless sales funnel.

Membership and Subscription Models

Building a community around your content opens the door to membership and subscription models. We explore the nuances of creating exclusive content for a paying audience. Learn how to build and sustain a community that values your expertise.

Challenges and Solutions in Content Creation

Overcoming Writer's Block

Writer's block is a common challenge for content creators. We provide practical tips and techniques to overcome writer's block and maintain a consistent content creation schedule. Discover how to tap into inspiration and creativity.

Managing Content Burnout

Consistent content creation can lead to burnout. We discuss strategies for managing burnout, from effective time management to incorporating breaks. Learn how to maintain a healthy balance between productivity and self-care.

Dealing with Negative Feedback

Negative feedback is an inevitable part of content creation. We guide you through constructive ways to handle criticism, learn from feedback, and turn challenges into opportunities for growth. Discover the resilience needed to navigate the online landscape.

SOCIAL MEDIA MONETIZATION TACTICS

In the unique scene of the computerized time, virtual entertainment has arisen as a force to be reckoned with for both individual articulation and pioneering adventures. This part is an inside and out investigation of web-based entertainment adaptation strategies, offering an exhaustive manual for transforming your social presence into a worthwhile road for money. From understanding the stages to carrying out viable systems, we dive into the complexities of utilizing online entertainment for monetary achievement.

Understanding the Landscape of Social Media

Changes in Social Media
Virtual entertainment stages have gone through a surprising development, molding the manner in which we interface and convey. We investigate the authentic improvement of online entertainment and how it has turned into a basic piece of the cutting edge computerized insight.

Social Media's Possibilities for Individuals
For people, web-based entertainment is in excess of a computerized jungle gym — it's a strong device for individual marking and pay age. We examine how virtual entertainment engages people to feature their ability, interface with crowds, and adapt their novel gifts.

Significant Online Entertainment Stages
An outline of the significant virtual entertainment stages lays the basis for successful adaptation techniques. From Facebook to Instagram, Twitter, LinkedIn, and arising stages, grasp the unmistakable elements and socioeconomics of every stage.

Building a Virtual Entertainment Presence

Making a Convincing Profile

Your online entertainment profile is the doorway to your crowd. We investigate the components of a convincing profile, from drawing in profile pictures to significant profiles. Figure out how to make a positive initial feeling that empowers crowd commitment.

Content Methodology for Web-based Entertainment
A clear cut content procedure is fundamental for online entertainment achievement. We dive into the subtleties of creating content that reverberates with your crowd. Learn how to create a social media presence that is engaging and cohesive, from caption strategies to visual elements.

Consistency and Recurrence
Consistency is the way to keeping a functioning and connected with crowd. We examine the significance of presenting recurrence and how on find some kind of harmony between remaining present and keeping away from content exhaustion.

Drawing in with Your Crowd
Online entertainment is a two-way road. We investigate powerful systems for drawing in with your crowd, from answering remarks to starting discussions. Figure out how to fabricate a local

area around your image and cultivate a feeling of association.

Adaptation Strategies via Online Entertainment

Force to be reckoned with Showcasing
Powerhouse promoting has turned into a worthwhile road for content makers. We investigate the elements of powerhouse showcasing, from teaming up with brands to arranging organizations. Comprehend how to situate yourself as an important powerhouse in your specialty.

Supported Content
On social media, sponsored content is an easy way to make money. We guide you through the method involved with getting supported open doors, from pitching to conveying excellent substance. Figure out how to flawlessly coordinate supported content into your feed while keeping up with realness.

Associate Showcasing via Online Entertainment
Affiliate marketing isn't limited to just one platform. We talk about viable techniques for carrying out subsidiary showcasing via virtual entertainment, from choosing important items to making enticing special substance. Open the capability of acquiring commissions through essential affiliations.

Selling Services and Goods

Your online entertainment crowd can be an immediate wellspring of income through item and administration deals. We investigate methodologies for selling your own items or administrations, from computerized items to stock. Figure out how to make a consistent deals pipe via online entertainment.

Stage Explicit Adaptation Techniques

Methods for Making Money on Instagram

Instagram offers extraordinary elements for adaptation. We investigate techniques, for example, supported posts, member promoting, and utilizing Instagram's shopping highlights. Learn how to get the most out of this platform focused on visuals.

Facebook Adaptation Strategies

Facebook offers numerous monetization options due to its large user base. We dig into techniques like Facebook Advertisements, supported posts, and using Facebook Gatherings for local area driven adaptation. Open the income streams that line up with the idea of the stage.

Twitter Adaptation Strategies

There are both challenges and opportunities associated with Twitter's real-time nature. We investigate methodologies, for example, supported tweets, partner promoting, and utilizing Twitter Spaces for direct commitment. Figure out how to explore the speedy universe of Twitter for compelling adaptation.

LinkedIn Adaptation Strategies
LinkedIn is an expert systems administration stage with unmistakable adaptation prospects. Utilizing LinkedIn's premium features and freelance opportunities are among the topics we discuss. Comprehend how to situate yourself as an idea chief and draw in business valuable open doors.

Building a Brand via Virtual Entertainment

Laying out Your Image Voice
Your image voice is the spirit of your web-based entertainment presence. We investigate how to characterize and lay out a steady brand voice that resounds with your crowd. Learn how to maintain professionalism while incorporating personality into your content.

Utilizing Visual Components

Visual components are crucial via web-based entertainment. We examine the significance of visual marking, from making a durable tasteful to using great pictures and illustrations. Comprehend how visual consistency upgrades memorability.

Strategies for Building a Community
Investing in your brand's community is a long-term strategy. We investigate techniques for local area working, from facilitating occasions to cultivating conversations. Figure out how to make a feeling of having a place that keeps your crowd effectively locked in.

Virtual Entertainment Difficulties and Arrangements

Managing Changes to the Algorithm
Virtual entertainment calculations are steadily evolving. We examine methodologies for exploring calculation refreshes, from remaining informed to adjusting your substance technique. Figure out how to limit the effect of calculation changes on your range.

Managing Savages and Negative Input
Negative input is an inescapable piece of online entertainment. We investigate valuable ways of

dealing with analysis, savages, and negative remarks. Find how to keep a positive internet based presence and explore testing circumstances with effortlessness.

Adjusting Individual and Expert
Adjusting individual and expert substance via online entertainment requires artfulness. We examine systems for keeping an expert picture while infusing individual components into your substance. Find out how to maintain a healthy balance for your brand.

Measurements and Investigation for Web-based Entertainment

KPIs, or key performance indicators, are:
It is essential to have an understanding of key performance indicators (KPIs) in order to measure the success of your social media efforts. Relevant metrics include reach, conversion, and engagement rates. Figure out how to decipher these measurements for informed navigation.

Tools for Social Media Analytics
Social media performance can be monitored using a variety of analytics tools. We examine famous devices and how to really use them. Learn how to

use data for continuous improvement, from native platform insights to third-party analytics.

An Iterative Growth Strategy
Virtual entertainment achievement is an iterative cycle. We investigate the significance of an iterative system for development, from refining content in view of examination to adjusting to advancing patterns. Figure out how to further develop your online entertainment presence constantly.

Legitimate and Moral Contemplations

Revelation and Straightforwardness
Keeping up with straightforwardness with your crowd is significant for moral web-based entertainment adaptation. We talk about the significance of divulgence in supported content and associate promoting. Learn how to communicate openly in order to build trust.

Rights in Intellectual Property
Regarding licensed innovation freedoms is central. We investigate the legal implications of creating and sharing content on social media. Figure out how to explore copyright issues and safeguard your own protected innovation.

Conformity with Platform Rules

Every web-based entertainment stage has its own arrangement of approaches. We examine the significance of consistence with stage rules to stay away from punishments or record limitations. Comprehend how to remain inside the limits of stage strategies while boosting adaptation potential open doors.

NETWORKING FOR PROFIT

Definition of Networking

Networking is more than exchanging business cards or connecting on LinkedIn; it's a dynamic process of building genuine relationships that extend beyond the superficial. In this section, we explore the true essence of networking and how it serves as a catalyst for both personal and professional growth.

The Evolution of Networking

The landscape of networking has evolved alongside technological advancements. We trace the evolution from traditional face-to-face networking to the digital age, where virtual connections and online platforms play a pivotal role. Understand how to navigate both realms for maximum impact.

Networking in the Digital Era

Digital platforms have transformed the way we connect. We delve into the nuances of networking in the digital era, exploring the advantages of online platforms, social media, and virtual events. Discover how to harness technology to expand your network and enhance profitability.

Building a Strategic Networking Mindset

The Strategic Importance of Networking

Networking is not a passive activity; it's a strategic investment in your professional journey. We discuss the critical importance of networking in today's competitive business landscape and how it contributes to profitability. Understand why strategic networking is a key driver of success.

Setting Clear Networking Goals

To navigate the vast landscape of networking opportunities, it's essential to set clear goals. We guide you through the process of defining your networking objectives, whether it's securing new clients, finding business partners, or gaining industry insights. Learn how to align your networking efforts with your broader business goals.

Identifying Your Unique Value Proposition

In a sea of professionals, standing out requires a clear understanding of your unique value proposition. We explore how to articulate your strengths, skills, and contributions in a way that captivates potential connections. Discover how to position yourself as a valuable asset in your network.

Strategies for Effective Networking

Strategic Networking Events

Attending networking events is a cornerstone of relationship-building. We discuss strategies for navigating both physical and virtual networking events. From conferences to industry meetups, learn how to make the most of these opportunities and forge meaningful connections.

Utilizing Online Platforms

Online platforms provide a wealth of networking opportunities. We explore strategies for leveraging platforms like LinkedIn, Twitter, and industry-specific forums. Understand how to optimize your profiles, engage with relevant content, and initiate connections that lead to profitable relationships.

The Power of Informational Interviews

Informational interviews offer a strategic avenue for networking. We guide you through the process of conducting informational interviews to gain insights, expand your network, and uncover potential opportunities. Learn how to approach professionals for these valuable conversations.

Networking through Professional Associations

Professional associations serve as hubs for industry-specific networking. We explore the benefits of joining associations, participating in events, and building connections with like-minded professionals. Discover how to leverage these networks for mutual growth.

Building Meaningful Connections

The Art of Effective Communication

Effective communication is the bedrock of successful networking. We delve into the art of crafting compelling introductions, engaging in meaningful conversations, and maintaining professional communication etiquette. Learn how to convey your message with clarity and impact.

Active Listening and Relationship Building

Networking is a two-way street that requires active listening. We discuss the importance of attentive listening, understanding the needs of your connections, and building relationships based on trust and reciprocity. Explore strategies for nurturing long-term connections.

Cultivating a Diverse Network

Diversity in your network adds richness and depth. We explore the benefits of cultivating a diverse network, from varied professional backgrounds to a mix of industries. Understand how diversity enhances creativity, expands opportunities, and contributes to profitability.

Networking for Profitable Opportunities

Identifying Business Opportunities

Profitable opportunities often arise from within your network. We guide you through the process of identifying potential business opportunities, whether it's partnerships, collaborations, or client referrals. Learn how to leverage your network as a source of revenue.

Securing New Clients through Networking

Client acquisition is a direct outcome of effective networking. We explore strategies for securing new clients through your network, from showcasing your expertise to referrals and testimonials. Understand how to position yourself as the go-to professional within your network.

Negotiating and Closing Deals

Effective networking extends to the negotiation and deal-closing phase. We discuss strategies for navigating negotiations, presenting proposals, and closing deals within your network. Learn how to approach these crucial stages with confidence and finesse.

Networking Challenges and Solutions

Overcoming Networking Anxiety

Networking anxiety is a common challenge. We provide practical tips and techniques for overcoming anxiety, whether it's at events, online platforms, or one-on-one interactions. Discover how to build confidence and navigate networking situations comfortably.

Dealing with Rejection

Rejection is an inherent part of networking. We explore constructive ways to handle rejection, learn from setbacks, and turn challenges into opportunities for growth. Understand the resilience needed to navigate rejection within the networking landscape.

Maintaining Authenticity

Authenticity is the linchpin of effective networking. We discuss the importance of staying true to yourself while navigating professional connections. Learn how to balance professionalism with authenticity and build genuine relationships that stand the test of time.

Metrics and Analytics for Networking

Key Performance Indicators (KPIs) for Networking

To measure the effectiveness of your networking efforts, understanding key performance indicators (KPIs) is crucial. We explore relevant metrics, from the growth of your network to the conversion of connections into opportunities. Learn how to track and interpret these metrics for continuous improvement.

Leveraging Networking Tools

Numerous tools are available to enhance your networking experience. We explore popular networking tools, from CRM software to virtual business cards. Understand how to leverage technology to streamline your networking efforts and stay organized.

Iterative Networking for Ongoing Success

Networking is an ongoing process of growth and refinement. We discuss the importance of an iterative networking strategy, from refining your approach based on analytics to adapting to evolving trends. Learn how to continuously improve your networking effectiveness.

Legal and Ethical Considerations

Confidentiality in Networking

Maintaining confidentiality is a cornerstone of ethical networking. We explore the importance of safeguarding sensitive information within your network and respecting the privacy of your connections. Understand how to navigate ethical considerations in networking.

Compliance with Anti-Spam Laws

In the digital age, compliance with anti-spam laws is crucial. We discuss the legal considerations of networking, from email communications to online interactions. Learn how to ensure compliance with regulations while building your network.

Professional Integrity in Networking

Professional integrity is non-negotiable in networking. We explore ethical considerations related to honesty, transparency, and accountability. Understand how to uphold a high standard of professional integrity in all your networking interactions.

LAUNCHING YOUR OWN PRODUCTS

Definition of Product Launch

Launching a product is more than presenting it to the market; it's a strategic process of creating anticipation, generating buzz, and ultimately positioning your product for success. In this section, we delve into the true essence of a product launch and its significance in the business landscape.

The Role of Product Launch in Business

A product launch is a pivotal moment that can define the trajectory of your business. We discuss how a well-executed launch goes beyond introducing a product; it establishes brand identity, captures market attention, and lays the foundation for sustained success.

Product Launch as a Strategic Business Decision

Launching a product is not a standalone event but a strategic decision intertwined with your overall business strategy. We explore how to align your product launch with your business goals, ensuring that it contributes to long-term growth and profitability.

Strategies for Successful Product Launch

Market Research and Validation

Market research is the bedrock of a successful product launch. We guide you through the process of conducting thorough market research, understanding customer needs, and validating your product concept. Learn how to ensure there's a demand for your offering before the launch.

Defining Your Target Audience

A deep understanding of your target audience is crucial for effective product positioning. We explore strategies for defining and segmenting your target audience, creating buyer personas, and tailoring your launch strategy to resonate with specific demographics.

Creating a Unique Value Proposition

In a crowded market, a compelling value proposition sets your product apart. We discuss the elements of a unique value proposition and guide you through the process of crafting a message that communicates the distinct benefits of your product to your audience.

Setting Clear Launch Goals

Clear goals are the foundation of a successful product launch. We explore how to set specific, measurable, and achievable launch goals that align with your overall business objectives. Understand the importance of defining metrics for success.

The Product Development Process

Idea Generation and Conceptualization

Every successful product begins with a compelling idea. We explore strategies for idea generation, from identifying market gaps to tapping into personal experiences. Learn how to conceptualize ideas and evaluate their feasibility for development.

Prototyping and Testing

Prototyping is a crucial step in the product development process. We guide you through the creation of prototypes, whether physical or digital, and discuss the importance of testing. Understand how to gather feedback, iterate on your design, and refine your product.

Product Design and Branding

Design and branding play a pivotal role in product perception. We delve into the principles of effective product design, from user experience to aesthetics. Explore strategies for creating a strong brand identity that resonates with your target audience.

Manufacturing and Production

For physical products, the manufacturing process is a critical aspect. We discuss strategies for choosing manufacturing partners, optimizing production processes, and ensuring quality control. Learn how to navigate the intricacies of bringing your product to life.

Creating Buzz Before Launch

Building a Pre-Launch Marketing Strategy

Generating anticipation before the launch is key to a successful product introduction. We explore strategies for building a pre-launch marketing plan, from teaser campaigns to exclusive previews. Learn how to create buzz and engage your audience before the product hits the market.

Utilizing Social Media Teasers

Social media is a powerful tool for creating excitement. We discuss strategies for leveraging social media platforms to release teasers, sneak peeks, and behind-the-scenes content. Understand how to build anticipation and foster a sense of community around your upcoming product.

Email Marketing for Pre-Launch Engagement

Building an email list allows you to directly engage with your audience. We explore strategies for using email marketing to generate interest before the launch. Learn how to craft compelling newsletters, offer exclusive content, and build a sense of exclusivity.

Engaging Influencers and Early Adopters

Influencers and early adopters can amplify your pre-launch efforts. We guide you through the process of identifying and engaging with influencers in your niche. Learn how to leverage their reach and credibility to build anticipation for your product.

The Launch Day and Beyond

Creating a Memorable Launch Event

The launch day is a pivotal moment that demands careful planning. We discuss strategies for creating a memorable launch event, whether physical or virtual. Explore the elements of a successful launch, from live demonstrations to exclusive offers.

Leveraging E-Commerce Platforms

E-commerce platforms provide a direct avenue to your audience. We explore strategies for leveraging platforms like Shopify, WooCommerce, or Amazon for your product launch. Learn how to optimize product listings, utilize e-commerce features, and maximize visibility.

Managing Inventory and Fulfillment

Effective inventory management is crucial for meeting demand. We guide you through strategies for managing inventory, selecting fulfillment partners, and ensuring a seamless shipping process. Learn how to avoid stockouts and provide a positive post-purchase experience.

Post-Launch Marketing and Promotion

The launch is just the beginning. We discuss strategies for post-launch marketing and promotion, from ongoing social media campaigns to email marketing. Understand how to maintain momentum, gather customer feedback, and iterate on your marketing strategy.

Customer Engagement and Support

Creating a Customer Support System

A robust customer support system is vital for post-launch success. We explore strategies for establishing customer support channels, responding to inquiries, and resolving issues. Learn how to create a positive and responsive customer experience.

Gathering and Utilizing Customer Feedback

Customer feedback is a valuable resource for product improvement. We discuss strategies for gathering feedback, whether through surveys, reviews, or direct communication. Understand how to use customer insights to iterate on your product and enhance future launches.

Implementing Customer Loyalty Programs

Building customer loyalty is an ongoing process. We explore strategies for implementing customer loyalty programs, from exclusive offers to rewards programs. Learn how to foster long-term relationships with your customer base.

Measuring Product Launch Performance:

Key Performance Indicators (KPIs) for Product Launch

To assess the success of your product launch, understanding key performance indicators (KPIs) is essential. We explore relevant metrics, from sales numbers to customer engagement and brand visibility. Learn how to track and interpret these metrics for informed decision-making.

Utilizing Analytics Tools for Product Launch

Analytics tools provide valuable insights into launch performance. We discuss popular analytics tools and how to leverage them effectively. From Google Analytics to e-commerce platform insights, understand how to harness data for continuous improvement.

Iterative Product Development and Launch Strategy

The launch is a stepping stone for future success. We discuss the importance of an iterative product development and launch strategy, from refining your approach based on analytics to adapting to evolving market trends. Learn how to continuously improve your product launches.

Legal and Ethical Considerations

Intellectual Property Protection

Protecting your intellectual property is paramount. We explore legal considerations related to patents, trademarks, and copyrights. Learn how to safeguard your product and brand from intellectual property infringement.

Compliance with Regulations

Products must adhere to industry regulations and standards. We discuss the importance of compliance with regulations, from safety standards to labeling requirements. Understand how to navigate regulatory considerations for a smooth product launch.

Ethical Marketing Practices

Ethical marketing is crucial for building trust with your audience. We explore ethical considerations in marketing, from transparent communication to avoiding deceptive practices. Learn how to maintain integrity throughout your product launch.

DOMINATING INTERNET BASED COURSES

Online courses have emerged as a powerful tool for learning and skill development in the rapidly changing educational landscape. This chapter provides insight, strategies, and useful advice for successfully navigating the digital learning environment and serves as a comprehensive guide to mastering online courses. From choosing the right courses to powerful concentrate on strategies and utilizing on the web assets, we investigate the diverse excursion of turning into an expert of online training.

Understanding the Value of Online Education

Meaning of Online Courses

Educational programs that are delivered through digital platforms are referred to as "online courses," "e-learning," or "digital courses." In this segment, we dive into the meaning of online courses and their extraordinary effect on customary schooling models.

The Advancement of Web based Learning

Internet learning has gone through a surprising development, formed by innovative progressions and the changing necessities of students. We follow the verifiable improvement of online instruction and investigate how it has turned into a standard and adaptable road for gaining information.

Internet Advancing as a Long lasting Undertaking

The idea of deep rooted learning is integral to online schooling. We examine the shift from conventional training designs to a persistent learning model worked with by online courses. Investigate the ways in which lifelong online learning encourages adaptability and skill growth.

Effective Online Learning Methods

Picking the Right Web-based Courses

Choosing the right internet based courses is a basic initial step. We investigate systems for recognizing courses that line up with your objectives, interests, and learning style. To make informed decisions, learn how to evaluate course content, instructor credentials, and user reviews.

Setting Clear Learning Goals

For focused and purposeful study, clear learning objectives are essential. We guide you through the most common way of defining explicit objectives for your web based learning venture, whether it's securing another expertise, acquiring a confirmation, or extending your insight in a specific subject.

Using time productively for Internet Learning

In the online learning environment, effective time management is essential. We examine procedures for making a review plan, overseeing cutoff times, and offsetting learning with different obligations. Comprehend how to enhance your time for most extreme efficiency.

Creating a Special Learning Environment

A helpful learning climate improves concentration and focus. We investigate procedures for making a devoted learning space, whether it's an actual room or a virtual work area. Figure out how to limit interruptions and cultivate a climate helpful for powerful learning.

Enhancing Online Study Methods

Dynamic Perusing and Note-Taking Systems

Dynamic perusing and note-taking are central review methods. We look at ways to interact with the course materials, take good notes, and remember what we learn. Find how to improve perception and review through dynamic perusing.

Viable Utilization of Media Assets

Online courses frequently integrate media components. We examine how to actually use recordings, introductions, and intuitive substance in your learning process. Recognize how multimedia enhances comprehension and accommodates various learning styles.

Taking Part in Online Conversations

Taking part in web-based conversations is a significant part of many courses. We investigate procedures for dynamic cooperation, deferential correspondence, and cooperative learning. Learn how to make meaningful contributions to discussions and gain insight from a variety of points of view.

Making use of LMS (Learning Management Systems)

In online education, Learning Management Systems (LMS) play a crucial role. We examine procedures for exploring and using LMS stages really. Learn how to use these systems to interact with instructors and peers, submit assignments, and access course materials.

Successful Correspondence in Web based Learning

Relationships with Instructors

It is essential for success to establish clear communication with instructors. We investigate methodologies for successful correspondence, from posing inquiries to looking for explanation. Figure out how to construct a positive compatibility with teachers and influence their mastery.

Working Together with Others

Cooperative learning is a sign of online instruction. We examine methodologies for teaming up with peers, partaking in bunch ventures, and cultivating a feeling of local area. Comprehend how to use aggregate information and advantage according to assorted viewpoints.

Looking for Help from Online People group

Online communities offer additional resources and support. We investigate systems for drawing in with online gatherings, conversation gatherings, and local area stages connected with your course. Figure out how to look for help, share bits of knowledge, and interface with similar students.

Surveying Learning Progress and Authority

Effective Preparation for Assessments

One important aspect of online learning is preparing for assessments. We talk about techniques for powerful evaluation planning, from investigating course materials to rehearsing with test questions. Comprehend how to move toward appraisals with certainty and preparation.

Using Self-Evaluation Apparatuses

Self-appraisal devices help in measuring your figuring out obviously happy. We investigate techniques for utilizing tests, self-evaluation modules, and intelligent activities. Learn how to tailor your study plan to your strengths and weaknesses.

Criticism Mix for Consistent Improvement

Input is a significant asset for development. We talk about techniques for incorporating input from educators, friends, and self-evaluation into your learning process. Comprehend how to utilize input productively and repeat on your review procedures.

Dominating Particular Abilities through Internet based Courses

Ability Improvement through Internet based Courses

Online courses are instrumental in expertise advancement. We investigate systems for dominating specific abilities, whether it's coding, visual communication, language capability, or some other range of abilities. Figure out how to structure your acquiring way for ability authority.

Building an Arrangement of Accomplishments

Recording your accomplishments is fundamental for displaying your abilities. We examine methodologies for building a portfolio that features your achievements, undertakings, and confirmations. Comprehend how to introduce your abilities actually to likely bosses or teammates.

Organizing Valuable open doors through Internet Learning

Web based learning gives organizing amazing open doors. We investigate systems for interfacing with educators, industry experts, and individual students. Figure out how to use web based systems administration to grow your expert associations and investigate vocation amazing open doors.

Using Extra Assets for Advanced Learning

Enhancing On the web Courses with Books and Articles

Online course materials are complemented by articles and books. We talk about methodologies for enhancing your learning with extra perusing. Comprehend how to choose significant books and articles that extend how you might interpret course ideas.

Investigating Internet Learning Stages and MOOCs

Internet learning reaches out past individual courses. To help you learn more, we discuss methods for exploring Massive Open Online Courses (MOOCs) and online learning platforms. Figure out how to get to courses from different establishments and expand your growth opportunity.

Webinars and workshops for ongoing education

Workshops and webinars provide opportunities for ongoing education. We examine systems for going to live meetings, online courses, and virtual studios. Comprehend how to remain refreshed on industry drifts and draw in with specialists in your field of study.

Overcoming Obstacles in Online Education

Tending to Specialized Difficulties

Specialized difficulties are normal in web based learning. We talk about ways to deal with problems like software bugs, device compatibility, and internet connectivity. Figure out how to investigate specialized difficulties and guarantee a smooth growth opportunity.

Overseeing Internet Learning Weakness

Internet learning weariness can affect inspiration and concentration. We look into ways to deal with exhaustion, keep enthusiasm, and avoid burnout. Comprehend how to figure out some kind of harmony among learning and taking care of oneself.

Adapting to Disconnection in Web based Learning

The potential for segregation is a test in web-based training. We examine methodologies for adapting to sensations of seclusion, cultivating a feeling of local area, and interfacing with individual students. In the online learning environment, learn how to build a support system.

Lawful and Moral Contemplations

Regarding Copyright and Scholastic Respectability

Regarding copyright and scholastic honesty is vital in web based learning. We investigate methodologies for staying away from counterfeiting, referring to sources accurately, and sticking to moral norms. Comprehend the results of scholarly unfortunate behavior and the significance of keeping up with trustworthiness.

Information Protection and Security in Web based Learning

Information protection and security are basic contemplations. We examine methodologies for shielding your own data, figuring out stage protection arrangements, and utilizing secure associations. Figure out how to explore the computerized scene with an emphasis on security.

Conformity with the Rules and Policies of the Course

Each web-based course has its own arrangement of approaches and rules. We talk about the significance of consistence, from complying with task time constraints to complying to course runs the show. Comprehend how to explore course strategies and add to a positive learning climate.

OUTSOURCING INSIGHT

Definition of Freelancing

Freelancing is a form of self-employment where individuals offer their skills and services to clients on a project-by-project basis. In this section, we delve into the definition of freelancing and its transformative impact on traditional employment structures.

The Rise of the Freelance Economy

The freelance economy has witnessed significant growth, driven by technological advancements and changing attitudes towards work. We explore the rise of freelancing, its impact on traditional employment models, and the advantages it offers to both freelancers and clients.

Freelancing as a Lifestyle Choice

Freelancing goes beyond a career; it's a lifestyle choice that offers flexibility and autonomy. We discuss how freelancing aligns with the desire for work-life balance, creative freedom, and the pursuit of personal and professional fulfillment.

Building a Successful Freelance Business:

Identifying Your Niche and Skills

Success in freelancing begins with identifying your niche and skills. We explore strategies for pinpointing your expertise, assessing market demand, and aligning your skills with client needs. Learn how to carve a niche that sets you apart in the competitive freelancing landscape.

Creating a Compelling Freelance Brand

A strong freelance brand is essential for attracting clients. We delve into strategies for creating a compelling brand identity, from a professional portfolio to a distinct online presence. Understand how to showcase your skills and communicate your unique value proposition.

Setting Freelance Business Goals

Clear business goals are the foundation of a successful freelancing career. We guide you through the process of setting specific, measurable, and achievable goals. Learn how to align your freelance business objectives with your long-term vision.

Establishing a Professional Online Presence

An online presence is a freelancer's storefront. We explore strategies for establishing a professional online presence through platforms like personal websites, social media, and freelance marketplaces. Understand how to optimize your profiles for maximum visibility.

Client Acquisition and Management

Strategies for Finding Freelance Clients

Client acquisition is a continuous process in freelancing. We discuss strategies for finding freelance clients, from leveraging online platforms to networking and referrals. Learn how to create a steady stream of client opportunities.

Effective Communication with Clients

Clear communication is vital for successful freelancing relationships. We explore strategies for effective communication with clients, from initial inquiries to project updates. Understand how to set expectations, ask clarifying questions, and build rapport with clients.

Negotiation and Pricing Strategies

Negotiation and pricing skills are integral to freelancing success. We delve into strategies for negotiating contracts, setting fair prices, and communicating the value of your services. Learn how to strike a balance between competitive pricing and fair compensation.

Client Relationship Management

Building long-term relationships with clients is a hallmark of freelancing success. We discuss strategies for client relationship management, from delivering exceptional work to staying proactive and responsive. Understand how to cultivate client loyalty and foster repeat business.

Optimizing Freelance Workflow

Effective Time Management for Freelancers

Time management is a critical aspect of freelancing. We explore strategies for effective time management, from creating schedules to prioritizing tasks. Learn how to optimize your workflow to meet deadlines and deliver high-quality work.

Utilizing Freelance Tools and Platforms

Freelance tools and platforms streamline business operations. We discuss essential tools, from project management software to invoicing platforms. Understand how to leverage technology to enhance your efficiency and professionalism.

Managing Multiple Freelance Projects

Handling multiple projects concurrently is common in freelancing. We explore strategies for managing multiple freelance projects, from setting realistic timelines to balancing workloads. Learn how to maintain quality and meet client expectations across various assignments.

Freelance Project Collaboration

Collaboration with other freelancers or specialists is a valuable aspect of freelancing. We discuss strategies for effective project collaboration, from communication tools to collaborative platforms. Understand how to create a seamless workflow when working with others.

Financial Management and Freelance Taxes

Financial Planning for Freelancers

Financial planning is crucial for freelancers' stability. We explore strategies for financial planning, including budgeting, saving, and managing irregular income. Learn how to create a financial cushion and navigate the financial aspects of freelancing.

Understanding Freelance Taxes

Freelance taxes require careful consideration. We delve into strategies for understanding freelance taxes, from tracking income and expenses to navigating deductions. Understand how to comply with tax regulations and optimize your financial position.

Invoicing and Payment Best Practices

Smooth invoicing and payment processes are essential for cash flow. We discuss best practices for invoicing, setting payment terms, and following up on payments. Learn how to maintain professionalism in financial transactions.

Building a Freelance Emergency Fund

An emergency fund is a freelancer's safety net. We explore strategies for building a freelance emergency fund, from setting aside a percentage of income to managing unexpected expenses. Understand how to create financial resilience in your freelancing career.

Adapting to the Freelance Landscape

Navigating Industry Changes and Trends

The freelance landscape is dynamic, with industry changes and trends shaping opportunities. We discuss strategies for navigating these shifts, staying informed, and adapting your skills to evolving demands. Learn how to position yourself as a forward-thinking freelancer.

Continuous Learning and Skill Development

Continuous learning is a key driver of freelance success. We explore strategies for ongoing skill development, from taking online courses to staying abreast of industry advancements. Understand how to stay competitive in a rapidly changing freelancing landscape.

Balancing Work and Personal Life

Maintaining a healthy work-life balance is crucial for freelancer well-being. We discuss strategies for balancing work and personal life, setting boundaries, and preventing burnout. Learn how to foster a sustainable and fulfilling freelance lifestyle.

Freelance Networking and Community Building

Networking is a powerful tool in freelancing. We explore strategies for freelance networking and community building, from online platforms to local events. Understand how to build professional connections, share insights, and collaborate within the freelance community.

Freelance Challenges and Solutions

Dealing with Scope Creep

Scope creep is a common challenge in freelancing. We discuss strategies for managing scope creep, setting clear boundaries, and communicating effectively with clients. Learn how to protect your time and deliver value within agreed-upon parameters.

Handling Client Disputes

Client disputes can arise in freelancing. We explore strategies for handling client disputes professionally and amicably. Understand how to navigate disagreements, find resolution paths, and maintain your professional reputation.

Coping with Freelance Isolation

Isolation is a potential challenge for freelancers. We discuss strategies for coping with freelance isolation, from joining online communities to engaging in co-working spaces. Learn how to build a support system and combat feelings of loneliness.

Legal and Ethical Considerations

Freelance Contract Essentials

A robust freelance contract is essential for clear expectations. We explore essential elements of freelance contracts, from project details to payment terms. Understand how to create contracts that protect both you and your clients.

Intellectual Property and Rights

Understanding intellectual property rights is crucial in freelancing. We discuss strategies for protecting your work and respecting client rights. Learn how to navigate intellectual property considerations to ensure a fair and ethical freelance practice.

Maintaining Professional Integrity

Professional integrity is non-negotiable in freelancing. We explore ethical considerations related to honesty, transparency, and accountability. Understand how to uphold a high standard of professional integrity in all your freelancing interactions.

UNDERSTANDING THE ART OF NEGOTIATION

Navigating Collaborative Discourse:

Negotiation transcends a mere exchange; it's a dynamic process of discussion and compromise to forge a shared agreement. Its essence lies in finding common ground, nurturing collaboration, and ensuring a symbiotic value exchange.

Essential Principles of Effective Negotiation:

Strategic Preparation:

1. The bedrock of successful negotiations is meticulous preparation. Knowing your goals, anticipating challenges, and understanding the other party's needs lay the groundwork for a fruitful discussion.

Attuned Listening:

2. Listening becomes a potent tool in negotiation. Beyond words, attentive listening builds rapport, fostering an environment where mutual understanding can thrive.

Transparent Dialogue:

3. Clear articulation of needs, expectations, and constraints sets the stage for successful negotiations. Transparency builds trust and facilitates collaborative problem-solving.

Flexibility and Creativity:

4. Rigidity has no place in negotiation. Being open to innovative solutions and adapting your approach to the context can lead to

creative compromises that satisfy both parties.

Patience and Persistence:

5. Negotiations are often a journey, not a sprint. Patience is a virtue, and persistent commitment to the process is vital for navigating challenges and reaching optimal outcomes.

Diverse Negotiation Landscapes:

Distributive Negotiation:

1. In this scenario, resources are finite, and parties vie for their share—a classic win-lose situation.

Integrative Negotiation:

2. A collaborative approach where both parties work together to maximize outcomes, focusing on creating value and expanding the resource pie.

Compromise:

3. Seeking middle ground through mutual concessions, compromise aims for a balanced solution that accommodates both parties' needs.

Pricing Strategies for Freelancers and Entrepreneurs:

Precision in Pricing:

Holistic Cost Understanding:

1. Delving into direct and indirect costs associated with your service or product is imperative. This encompasses time, materials, and overhead.

Market Savvy:

2. A keen understanding of the market landscape ensures informed pricing

decisions. Researching comparable services or products aids in competitive positioning.

Value-Driven Pricing:

3. Going beyond mere cost considerations, value-based pricing centers on the perceived value of your offering to the customer, emphasizing impact and outcomes.

Varied Pricing Models:

Hourly Rate:

1. Common in service-oriented fields, this model charges clients based on the hours invested, aligning effort with value.

Project-Based Pricing:

2. A fixed fee for the entire project is suitable when the scope of work is well-defined and unlikely to significantly change.

Retainer Model:

3. Offering clients a recurring fee for ongoing services ensures stability and predictability for both parties.

Value-Based Pricing:

4. This approach ties pricing to the perceived value of your service to the client, focusing on outcomes rather than time invested.

Factors Influencing Pricing Decisions:

Market Demand Assessment:

1. Evaluating demand for your services guides pricing strategies. High demand may support higher prices, while oversaturation may necessitate competitive rates.

Client Budget Alignment:

2. Harmonizing your pricing with the client's budget ensures accessibility and aligns your offerings with their financial expectations.

Competitive Landscape Analysis:

3. Understanding how your pricing compares to competitors provides context and helps position your offerings strategically.

Industry Standards Awareness:

4. Familiarity with industry benchmarks provides a baseline for pricing decisions, ensuring competitiveness in the market.

Negotiation Techniques for Freelancers and Entrepreneurs:

Building Rapport:

Establishing Personal Connections:

1. Initiating negotiations with personal touches through small talk creates a relaxed atmosphere, laying the groundwork for rapport.

Identifying Common Ground:

2. Discovering shared interests fosters collaboration and sets a positive tone for negotiations.

Effective Communication:

Articulating Value Clearly:

1. Clearly communicating the value of your services aids the other party in understanding the benefits they stand to gain.

Open-Ended Questioning:

2. Encouraging dialogue through open-ended questions deepens understanding, facilitating more effective negotiations.

Creating Win-Win Solutions:

Seeking Mutual Gains:

1. Identifying areas where both parties can benefit fosters a positive atmosphere, leading to mutually beneficial agreements.

Flexibility in Concessions:

2. Flexibility in making concessions, aligned with your priorities, demonstrates a collaborative spirit and contributes to a successful negotiation.

Overcoming Objections:

Proactive Problem-Solving:

1. Treating objections as opportunities for joint problem-solving transforms challenges into collaborative solutions.

Offering Alternatives:

2. Providing alternatives or compromises when faced with objections demonstrates flexibility and a genuine interest in finding solutions that satisfy both parties.

Negotiating Price:

Affirming Your Value:

Confidence in Your Worth:

1. Confidence in your skills and the value you bring is crucial, not just for your negotiation stance but also to convey assurance to the other party.

Understanding Client Budgets:

2. Gathering information about your client's budget before negotiations allows you to tailor discussions to their financial expectations.

Techniques for Pricing Negotiations:

Anchor Pricing:

1. Starting with a higher price as an anchor, even if anticipating negotiation, sets a

reference point influencing perceptions of value.

Bundling and Unbundling:

2. Offering bundled services or unbundling for a modular approach provides flexibility in meeting client needs.

Navigating Common Pricing Challenges:

Scope Creep Mitigation:

Clear Scope Definition:

1. Clearly defining the scope of work in initial agreements helps prevent scope creep. Additional work outside this scope should be addressed separately, with clear terms and pricing.

Change Order Process:

2. Implementing a change order process formalizes modifications, ensuring both parties agree on changes and associated costs.

Addressing Budget Constraints:

Providing Options:

1. Offering different service or product options at varying price points allows clients to choose a package aligning with their budget.

Phased Approaches:

2. Breaking down larger projects into phased approaches accommodates budget constraints and offers flexibility in project planning.

SCALING YOUR INSIGHT BUSINESS

Defining Scaling in the Knowledge Economy:

Scaling, in the context of a knowledge business, goes beyond mere expansion; it involves systematically increasing your capacity to handle growth without compromising the quality and value of your offerings. It's about creating a sustainable framework that accommodates a growing audience while maintaining excellence.

Importance of Scaling:

Meeting Increased Demand:

1. As your knowledge business gains traction, the demand for your expertise and insights is likely to grow. Scaling ensures that you can meet this demand efficiently.

Enhancing Profitability:

2. A well-executed scaling strategy can lead to increased profitability by optimizing operations, reaching new markets, and diversifying revenue streams.

Establishing Authority and Impact:

3. Scaling allows you to amplify your influence and establish authority in your niche. A larger audience base enhances your impact on industry trends and thought leadership.

Creating Long-Term Sustainability:

4. By developing scalable systems, you ensure the long-term sustainability of your knowledge business. This resilience is vital in the face of evolving market conditions.

Strategies for Scaling Your Knowledge Business:

1. Systematizing Your Processes:

a. Content Production and Delivery:

Content Calendar and Workflow:

- Establish a content calendar to streamline your content production process. A well-defined workflow ensures consistency and quality.

Automation Tools:

- Explore automation tools for content distribution. This can include social media scheduling tools, email marketing platforms, and content management systems.

Scalable Learning Platforms:

- Invest in learning management systems (LMS) or online course platforms to deliver your knowledge products at scale. These platforms provide a structured and scalable way to share your expertise.

b. Client Onboarding and Support:

Standardized Onboarding Processes:

- Develop standardized onboarding processes for new clients or students. This ensures a smooth transition and sets clear expectations from the beginning.

Scalable Support Systems:

- Implement scalable support systems such as chatbots, FAQs, or a community forum to address common queries efficiently as your audience grows.

2. Leveraging Technology and Digital Platforms:

a. Online Presence and Branding:

Optimized Website:

- Ensure your website is optimized for scalability. This includes fast loading times, mobile responsiveness, and an intuitive user interface.

SEO and Digital Marketing:

- Invest in SEO strategies and digital marketing to expand your online reach. A well-executed digital presence is crucial for attracting a larger audience.

b. Data Analytics:

Utilizing Analytics Tools:

- Leverage analytics tools to gather insights into user behavior, content performance, and market trends. Data-driven decision-making is pivotal for effective scaling.

Personalization Strategies:

- Implement personalization strategies based on user data. Tailoring your offerings to individual preferences enhances user engagement and satisfaction.

3. Collaboration and Networking:

a. Partnerships and Collaborations:

Strategic Partnerships:

- Seek strategic partnerships with other experts, businesses, or platforms in your industry. Collaborative ventures can expand your reach and bring in diverse audiences.

Affiliate Marketing Programs:

- Implement affiliate marketing programs to encourage others to promote your knowledge products. This can exponentially increase your sales channels.

b. Community Building:

Online Communities:

- Establish and nurture online communities around your niche. This could be through social media groups, forums, or dedicated community platforms.

Engagement Strategies:

- Develop engagement strategies to keep your community active and involved. Regular interactions, discussions, and exclusive content can foster a sense of belonging.

4. Diversifying Revenue Streams:

a. Product Offerings:

Expanding Product Range:

- Introduce new knowledge products or services to diversify your offerings. This could include advanced courses, workshops, or consulting services.

Subscription Models:

- Explore subscription-based models for ongoing revenue. Subscription services can include premium content, exclusive access, or regular updates.

b. Monetization Strategies:

Adopting Various Monetization Channels:

- Implement a mix of monetization channels, such as one-time purchases, subscriptions, and freemium models. This flexibility accommodates different audience preferences.

Affiliate Marketing and Sponsorships:

- Incorporate affiliate marketing and sponsorships into your revenue model. Collaborating with relevant brands can provide additional income streams.

5. Talent Acquisition and Delegation:

a. Building a Team:

Identifying Skill Gaps:

- Identify areas where your expertise may be complemented by others. Building a team with diverse skills allows for a more comprehensive approach.

Outsourcing:

- Consider outsourcing tasks that can be handled more efficiently by specialists. This may include content creation, marketing, or technical aspects.

b. Delegating Responsibilities:

Effective Delegation:

- Develop a system for effective delegation of tasks. Clearly define roles and responsibilities to ensure smooth collaboration within your team.

Empowering Team Members:

- Empower team members to take ownership of specific aspects of your business. This fosters a sense of responsibility and encourages proactive contributions.

Real-World Case Studies:

1. MasterClass:

MasterClass, an online education platform, scaled by consistently attracting high-profile experts across various fields. By offering exclusive courses taught by celebrities and industry leaders, they created a unique value proposition, resulting in widespread popularity.

2. Coursera:

Coursera, a massive open online course (MOOC) platform, scaled by forming partnerships with universities and institutions globally. This collaborative approach allowed them to offer a diverse range of courses, expanding their reach and influence.

Challenges and Mitigation Strategies:

1. Quality Control:

Mitigation:

- Implement a robust quality control system. Regularly update and review content, seek feedback from users, and stay committed to delivering high-quality knowledge products.

2. Scalability of Support Systems:

Mitigation:

- Invest in scalable support systems, including chatbots, FAQs, and community forums. Prioritize user experience and ensure that support scales alongside your growing audience.

3. Team Dynamics and Communication:

Mitigation:

- Foster effective communication within your team. Utilize project management tools, conduct regular check-ins, and encourage an open and collaborative work culture.

4. Adapting to Market Changes:

Mitigation:

- Stay agile and adaptable. Regularly assess market trends, gather user feedback, and be willing to pivot your strategies to align with evolving demands.

REMAINING AHEAD IN THE INFORMATION ECONOMY

Defining the Knowledge Economy:

The knowledge economy is characterized by the predominant role of information, expertise, and intellectual capabilities in driving economic growth. In this paradigm, the creation, dissemination, and application of knowledge are pivotal contributors to innovation, productivity, and overall economic development.

Key Features of the Knowledge Economy:

Information as a Commodity:

1. In the knowledge economy, information is not just a resource; it's a valuable commodity. The ability to generate, curate, and utilize information strategically becomes a competitive advantage.

Rapid Technological Advances:

2. Technology is a driving force, facilitating the rapid creation and distribution of knowledge. Innovations such as artificial intelligence, big data analytics, and blockchain redefine how information is processed and utilized.

Focus on Intellectual Capital:

3. Intellectual capital, including human expertise and innovative ideas, takes center stage. Companies and individuals who invest in continuous learning and skill development gain a competitive edge.

Global Connectivity:

4. The knowledge economy transcends geographical boundaries. Global connectivity through the internet enables seamless collaboration, information exchange, and market access.

Strategies for Staying Ahead:

1. Embracing a Lifelong Learning Mindset:

a. Continuous Skill Development:
Identifying Emerging Skills:

- Regularly assess the skills in demand within your industry. Identify emerging trends and technologies that are shaping the future landscape.

Committing to Learning Paths:

- Embrace structured learning paths. Online courses, workshops, and certifications can provide a systematic approach to acquiring new skills.

b. Cultivating a Growth Mindset:
Embracing Challenges:

- View challenges as opportunities for growth. A growth mindset encourages resilience, adaptability, and a positive approach to learning from experiences.

Seeking Feedback:

- Actively seek feedback on your performance and be open to constructive criticism. Feedback is a valuable tool for refining skills and approaches.

2. Harnessing Technology for Innovation:

a. Tech Adoption and Adaptation:
Staying Informed on Tech Trends:

- Keep abreast of technological trends relevant to your field. Regularly explore emerging technologies and assess their potential impact.

Experimentation and Prototyping:

- Foster a culture of experimentation. Actively engage in prototyping and testing new technologies to understand their practical applications.

b. Leveraging Data for Insights:
Data-Driven Decision-Making:

- Embrace data-driven decision-making. Analyze data to gain insights into market trends, user behavior, and areas for improvement.

Investing in Analytics Tools:

- Invest in analytics tools that provide actionable insights. Tools for data visualization, predictive analytics, and market research can be invaluable.

3. Building a Robust Professional Network:

a. Networking Strategies:
Strategic Networking:

- Network strategically with professionals in your industry. Attend conferences, join online forums, and actively participate in discussions to broaden your connections.

Mentorship and Collaboration:

- Seek mentorship from experienced individuals in your field. Collaborate on projects and initiatives that allow for knowledge exchange and mutual growth.

b. Community Engagement:
Contributing to Communities:

- Actively contribute to professional communities. Share your insights, participate in discussions, and contribute to the collective knowledge pool.

Hosting Webinars and Workshops:

- Host webinars and workshops to share your expertise. This not only positions you as a thought leader but also provides opportunities for engagement.

4. Fostering Innovation and Creativity:

a. Cultivating a Culture of Innovation:
Encouraging Idea Generation:

- Foster an environment where team members feel empowered to share innovative ideas. Encourage brainstorming sessions and open dialogue.

Diversity and Inclusion:

- Recognize the value of diversity in fostering innovation. Embrace diverse perspectives, backgrounds, and experiences within your team.

b. Design Thinking Principles:
Adopting Design Thinking:

- Apply design thinking principles to problem-solving. This user-centric approach encourages creative solutions that address real user needs.

Iterative Prototyping:

- Implement iterative prototyping. Test and refine ideas through a series of prototypes, incorporating feedback at each stage.

5. Adapting to Market Dynamics:

a. Market Research and Trend Analysis:
Continuous Market Research:

- Conduct ongoing market research to stay informed about industry trends, competitor strategies, and shifts in consumer behavior.

Scenario Planning:

- Engage in scenario planning to anticipate potential future developments. Consider various scenarios and strategize for adaptability.

b. Agility in Decision-Making:
Agile Decision-Making Processes:

- Develop agile decision-making processes. The ability to make informed decisions swiftly is crucial in a dynamic knowledge economy.

Piloting New Initiatives:

- Pilot new initiatives on a smaller scale before full-scale implementation. This minimizes risks and allows for adjustments based on real-world feedback.

Case Studies in Staying Ahead:

1. Google:

Google maintains its position as a leader in the tech industry by fostering a culture of innovation. The company encourages employees to spend a portion of their work time on personal projects, leading to breakthroughs such as Gmail and Google Maps.

2. Elon Musk (Tesla, SpaceX):

Elon Musk stays ahead in both the automotive and aerospace industries by embracing technological advancements. Tesla's focus on electric vehicles and SpaceX's achievements in space exploration showcase Musk's commitment to pushing boundaries.

Overcoming Challenges:

1. Information Overload:

Curation and Prioritization:

- Develop curation strategies to manage information overload. Prioritize information relevant to your goals and industry.

Continuous Learning Platforms:

- Utilize continuous learning platforms that offer curated content. These platforms often use algorithms to recommend relevant resources.

2. Burnout and Work-Life Balance:

Setting Boundaries:

- Establish clear boundaries between work and personal life. Prioritize self-care and mental well-being to prevent burnout.

Delegating Responsibilities:

- Delegate tasks when necessary. Building a support system allows for efficient task delegation and reduces individual workload.

3. Technological Disruption:

Anticipating Disruptions:

- Stay informed about emerging technologies that may disrupt your industry. Anticipate potential disruptions and proactively adjust strategies.

Agile Technological Adoption:

- Develop an agile approach to adopting new technologies. Test and integrate technologies gradually to minimize disruption.